SKATING SUPERSTARS

With 16
full-color poster
photos of
top stars

ALLISON GERTRIDGE

FIREFLY BOOKS

*I'd like to dedicate this book to the mothers: mothers who
woke their skaters at four in the morning and taxied them to and from
the rink; mothers who worked overtime at second (and third!) jobs to pay for coaching
fees; mothers who knew just what to say when the going got tough. And to one mother
in particular, who has always encouraged me.*

—A.J.G.

*Special thanks to Barb Wilson at the Canadian Figure Skating Association
and to all of the skaters who took the time to do interviews for this book.
Without your help, this project would never have happened.*

Photo credits:

Courtesy CANAPRESS Photo Service:
O. Baiul (Paul Chiasson), P. Candeloro (Wide World Photos), L. Chen (Paul Chiasson),
N. Kerrigan (Paul Chiasson), A. Urmanov (Wide World Photos), K. Yamaguchi (Philip Walker).

Courtesy the Canadian Figure Skating Association:
Bourne/Kraatz (F. Scott Grant), Brasseur/Eisler (Gerry Thomas), S. Britten (F. Scott Grant),
K. Browning (F. Scott Grant), J. Chouinard (Gerry Thomas),S. Humphreys (F. Scott Grant),
K. Preston (F. Scott Grant), Jennifer Robinson (F. Scott Grant),
Sargeant/Wirtz (F. Scott Grant), E. Stojko (Gerry Thomas).

Courtesy PMA: Michelle Kwan (Cindy Lang)

Cover photo of Michelle Kwan courtesy PMA/Irene Erseck

A FIREFLY BOOK

Published 1996 in the United States by:

Firefly Books (U.S) Inc.
P.O. Box 1383
Ellicott Station
Buffalo, New York
14207

Cataloguing in Publication Data

Gertridge, Allison
Skating superstars

ISBN 1-55209-009-4

1. Skaters - Biography - Juvenile literature.
2. Skaters - Canada - Biography - Juvenile literature.
3. Skating - Juvenile literature.   4. Skating - Canada -
Juvenile literature. I. Title.

GV850.A2G47 1996   j796.91'2'0922   C96-930442-0

Printed and bound in Canada

∞ ABOUT THE JUMPS ∞

Did you know that...

Figure skating blades are concave? They have two sharp edges with a hollow in the middle. Skaters use different parts of their blades — inside or outside edge, front or back — to push off and complete different moves. Jumps in which skaters use their picks are called toe-assisted jumps.

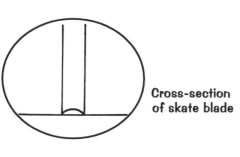

Cross-section
of skate blade

AXEL

Named after its creator, Axel Paulsen, this is the hardest jump of all. An Axel is the only jump that skaters begin by going forward and the only one that requires them to do an extra half-rotation. For example, a double Axel is actually two and a half turns. Moving forward, skaters take off from the front outside edge of one skate, rotate and land on the outside edge of the opposite foot, moving backwards.

FLIP

For this jump, skaters take off from the back inside edge of one skate, pushing off with the toe of the opposite foot. They land on the back outside edge of the skate used for the toe-assist.

LOOP

Skaters take off from the back outside edge of one skate, turn and land on the same back outside edge.

LUTZ

The Lutz jump requires a lot of power. Skaters take off from the back outside edge of their left skate while pushing off with their right toe. Then they turn counter-clockwise before landing on the back outside edge of the right foot.

SALCHOW

This jump was named after its creator, ten-time world champion Ulrich Salchow (pronounced *sol-cow*) of Sweden. To do it, skaters take off from the back inside edge of one skate, bringing their free leg forward to begin the spin and without pushing off with a toe. Skaters then land on the back outside edge of their skate. [Not shown.]

TOE LOOP

Usually performed as a double or a triple, this jump was invented by Werner Rittberger. In a toe loop skaters take off from the back outside edge of one skate, pushing off and up with the toe of the free foot. Then they turn and land on the back outside edge of the skate they started with.

Oksana Baiul

OKSANA BAIUL

When she was a child, Oksana Baiul wanted to be a ballerina, so her grandfather bought her a pair of skates to help her slim down and get fit. In 1993, still a child at 15, a graceful Oksana made her first appearance at the world championships and won a gold medal — the youngest to do so since Sonja Henie.

Oksana's father disappeared when she was two years old, and her mother died of cancer in 1991, leaving Oksana an orphan at the age of 13. She lived with her first coach, Stanislav Koretek, until he moved to Canada in 1992, and then found a family and coach in Galina Zmievskaya.

Galina speaks highly of Oksana: "God has taken away her family, but the skating world is now her family. It's all natural to her, all God-given talent. You tell her something and she goes, 'Like this?' She does it all on her own."

Galina is also the coach and mother-in-law of Viktor Petrenko, Oksana's friend and 1992 world and Olympic champion in men's singles. Until recently, Viktor was paying for Oksana's skates and costumes because she barely had enough money of her own to pay for necessities.

Then came Oksana's first Olympic Games. The day before she was to skate her long program, Oksana collided with a German skater in a practice session. She needed three stitches to close the cut on her leg and two painkilling injections the next day to get her through the program. Oksana two-footed the landing of her triple flip, but more than made up for her mistake when she risked an extra triple jump near the end of her program. Oksana won the gold.

Praised for her dynamic spins and intricate footwork, it's Oksana's winning smile people seem to remember most. In fact, one judge has admitted that her facial expressions sometimes make it difficult to remember to look at her feet!

One shouldn't be afraid to lose; this is sport. One day you win; another day you lose. Of course, everyone wants to be the best. This is normal. This is what sport is about. This is why I love it.
— Oksana

Born:
November 16, 1977

In:
Dnepropetrovsk, Ukraine

Height:
160 cm (5'4")

Weight:
43 kg (95 lbs)

Coach:
Galina Zmievskaya

Category:
Ladies' singles

Status:
Professional

Highlights

1st at Olympic Games (1994)

1st at World Championships (1993)

2nd at European Championships (1993)

1st at national championships (1992)

Bourne / Kraatz

SHAE-LYNN BOURNE
and
VICTOR KRAATZ

Shae-Lynn Bourne and Victor Kraatz — also known as Crash and Burn — are the hottest, fastest rising duo in ice skating. And they've introduced some great new moves to their sport. After a captivating demonstration on the Olympic warm-up rink, people from as far away as Bermuda were talking about those Canadian ice dancers who did that incredible "hydroblading."

Hydroblading is a kind of skating that Victor and Shae-Lynn use to help them become comfortable skating on the edge of their blades at angles of 45° or less. Using a pylon for support, they keep their bodies absolutely straight and skate really low to the ice. Although pylons aren't permitted in competition, the pair still manages to incorporate some hydroblading into its routines by "using each other like a pylon," as Shae-Lynn describes it.

Every year the requirements of the original dance program change. Each year, Victor and Shae-Lynn work at learning the dance they are expected to use. "It's just like how an actor who has to play a police officer goes to the police station to find out something about it," says Victor.

Although ice dancers are prohibited from doing the dangerous jumps and throws that pairs skaters include in their programs, Shae-Lynn and Victor have learned that their sport is not without its risks. Once, while working on a particularly difficult lift, Shae-Lynn's hair came undone and touched the ice. Victor had no choice but to skate over it, cutting off eight centimetres of hair as he did. Shae-Lynn laughs, though, when she recalls how she got her revenge — later that day when another lift went wrong, she accidentally kicked him in the nose with her toe pick!

A lot of skaters want the audience to cheer them on. We give all we have to excite the audience and to light them up and then at the end, hopefully, we'll get the applause.
— Shae-Lynn and Victor

Born:
January 24, 1976
April 7, 1971

In:
Chatham, Ontario
Berlin, Germany

Height:
159 cm (5′4″)
178 cm (5′11″)

Weight:
52 kg (114 lbs)
70 kg (155 lbs)

Coaches:
Marina Klimova,
Sergei
Ponomarenko

Category:
Ice Dancing

Status:
Amateur, Canada

Highlights

4th at World
Championships
(1995)

6th at World
Championships
(1994)

10th at Olympic
Games (1994)

1st at Canadian
Championships
(1993, 1994, 1995,
1996)

1st at Canadian
Junior
Championships
(1992)

Brasseur / Eisler

ISABELLE BRASSEUR
and
LLOYD EISLER

In the beginning they didn't even speak the same language. And on top of that, after taking one look at Lloyd Eisler, shy Isabelle Brasseur decided she would have nothing to do with him. His age — he's seven years older — and the fact that he's so much bigger than she is — he's 28 centimetres taller — had her worried that she might get hurt. But after only two days of skating together, fear was the farthest thing from Isabelle's mind. Soon she thought nothing of being tossed nearly four metres in the air!

Brasseur and Eisler's trademark move is a triple lateral twist, in which Isabelle is thrown into the air and spins three times before being caught. But it wasn't just powerful moves that finally won this team their dream gold. Isabelle, along with choreographer Uschi Keszler and coach Josée Picard, persuaded Lloyd to try a more graceful approach in their routine. The adjustment suited Isabelle's softer style well and it won them first place at the 1993 World Championships.

Isabelle knows that Lloyd can sometimes give people the impression that he's a pretty mean guy — if he performs badly he lets the world know how upset he is with himself! But she also knows how kind Lloyd can be. After all, he was there to support her when her father died unexpectedly in 1992. Isabelle once said in an interview, "People don't really see what he does for me outside the ice. All the time something happens, he's the one I go to, and he's the one who is going to take care of me. . . . "

On July 25, 1994, Olympic bronze medalists and five-time Canadian champions, Isabelle and Lloyd retired from amateur competitions. But they didn't drop out of sight. Fans continue to be thrilled as one of Canada's best teams ever takes on a host of charities and a heart-pounding tour of the professional circuit.

Did you know that . . .?
Before they were paired together,
Isabelle and Lloyd had already successfully
competed as pairs skaters with different partners?

Born:
July 28, 1970
April 28, 1963

In:
Kingsbury, Quebec
Seaforth, Ontario

Height:
150 cm (5′)
178 cm (5′11″)

Weight:
44 kg (96 lbs)
82 kg (180 lbs)

Coaches:
Josée Picard
Eric Gillies

Category:
Pairs

Status:
Professional

Highlights

1st at World
Championships
(1993)

3rd at Olympic
Games (1992, 1994)

2nd at World
Championships
(1990, 1991, 1994)

7th at World
Championships
(1989)

1st at Canadian
Championships
(1989, 1991, 1992,
1993, 1994)

9th at Olympic
Games (1988)

Sébastien Britten

SÉBASTIEN BRITTEN

Sébastien Britten does not come from a skating family — neither of his two brothers skates. But with a star like Sébastien in the family, one might be enough!

Sébastien has been training with coach Josée Normand since he was eleven years old. As well as practicing on the ice with choreographers Jean Pierre Boulais and David Wilson, he also does strength training exercises. And he takes ballet classes with Jean Hughes Rochette from Les Grands Ballets Canadiens. This competitor works hard — and it has paid off.

Sébastien was Canadian junior champion in 1990, and senior bronze medallist in 1992 and again in 1994. That third-place finish qualified him for a spot on the 1994 Olympic team in Lillehammer.

Making it to the Olympics was a big thrill for Sébastien. But things started off badly. In the weeks leading up to the Games, he developed a bad case of bronchitis. It got worse and worse until the competition began. Before he skated Sébastien was actually given oxygen to help him breathe through the congestion. But his strength and training came through, and he finished his routine. Incredibly, he finished tenth — at a time when most people would never have gotten out of bed!

With Kurt Browning's move to the professional ranks in 1994, Sébastien became the second-ranked skater in Canada. And when Elvis Stojko's injured leg kept him from competing at the Canadian Championships the next year, Sébastien won his first-ever senior nationals. With his talent and drive — and with the all-important triple axel added to his program — we should see Sébastien Britten on the winner's podium for years to come.

Did you know that . . .?
Choreographers must have a valid first-aid certificate before they can work with Canadian skaters. Often they're the only people around when a skater takes a bad fall.

Born:
May 17, 1970

In:
Verdun, Quebec

Height:
170 cm (5'8")

Weight:
64 kg (140 lbs)

Coach:
Josée Normand

Category:
Men's singles

Status:
Amateur, Canada

Highlights

2nd at Canadian Championships (1996)

1st at Canadian Championships (1995)

8th at World Championships (1994)

10th at Olympic Games (1994)

4th at Canadian Championships (1993)

3rd at Canadian Championships (1992, 1994)

1st at Canadian Junior Championships (1990)

Kurt Browning

KURT BROWNING

Why did four-time world champion Kurt Browning first take up figure skating? So he could become a better hockey player, of course! Luckily, it wasn't long before slapshots gave way to Axel jumps.

He has taken first place at four Canadian and four World Championships. And on March 25, 1988, Kurt spun his way into *The Guinness Book of Records* by becoming the first skater ever to do a quadruple jump in competition.

In fact, just about the only thing this super-talented skater *hasn't* done is win an Olympic medal — something he was determined to do in 1992 before going on tour with friend Kristi Yamaguchi. But a back injury took eight weeks out of Kurt's training program that year. He had to skip the 1992 Canadians all together and only came in sixth at the Albertville Olympics.

So, Kurt set his sights on the 1994 Games in Lillehammer. He changed coaches and began a weight-training program to build muscle in his upper body.

At the 1994 Games, Kurt skated a heart-breaking short program, making so many mistakes that he fell to 12th place. But he had a sure-to-please long program ready to go. Dressed in a white tux and tails, Kurt was a debonair Humphrey Bogart, skating to the music "As Time Goes By." Kurt's weight-training program had made his back better able to support his excellent jumps, and his performance was superb. Kurt wowed the judges and jumped to fifth place!

Although he didn't win that particular gold, Kurt did get a chance to see just how supportive his Canadian "family" is. Fans from across the country sent in gold watches and jewelry (even gold teeth!) to make Kurt a special thank-you medal. On it were the words, *From all the hearts you've captured.* After years of hard work and crowd-pleasing performances, Kurt Browning earned his gold.

Before I step off the ice, I want to leave an impression with the audience. I want to make them feel a little bit better than they did before. . . . If what I do stays with them longer than the moment, I've succeeded.

— Kurt

Born:
June 18, 1966

In:
Rocky Mountain House, Alberta

Height:
168 cm (5'6")

Weight:
66 kg (145 lbs)

Coach:
Louis Stong

Category:
Men's singles

Status:
Professional

Highlights

5th at Olympic Games (1994)

1st at World Championships (1989, 1990, 1991, 1993)

1st at Canadian Championships (1989, 1990, 1991, 1993)

8th at Olympic Games (1988)

2nd at Canadian Championships (1987, 1988, 1994)

5th at Canadian Championships (1986)

Philippe Candeloro

PHILIPPE CANDELORO

Who else would do a striptease before his program but gutsy French skater Philippe Candeloro! With costumes that range from showy to outrageous, this heartthrob has had one or two run-ins with skating officials over regulation dress. They've had their disagreements about his routines, too, as Candeloro's dazzling trademark move involves spinning not on the blades of his skates, but on his ankles!

In rusty English Philippe explains, "It's dangerous for the knees and ligaments. You need to have flexible ligaments. If not, you can have problems. You have to see how I do it. Some guys in France had problems after they tried my spin."

Despite his fantastic stage presence and jumping ability, Philippe has had trouble scoring points with judges for style. He says, "I had very bad artistic impression. I didn't like artistry. For me it seems like it was for a girl. All my friends, the guys I go out with, say to me, 'You do a sport for girls.' If it's for guys you have to jump. Dance is not good."

But with the help of choreographer Natacha Dabbadie, and a slight change in attitude, Philippe has been working on the dance portion of his programs. And it certainly has made a difference to his scores.

At the 1994 Olympics, in a tribute to his Italian-born father, Philippe skated to music from the "Godfather" movies. And although he fell on a difficult triple Axel near the end of his long program, Philippe was able to show off some of his new footwork to bring in a bronze medal.

Says Philippe, "Now I skate what I want and everybody likes what I do."

Born:
February 17, 1972

In:
Courbevoie, France

Height:
172 cm (5'9")

Weight:
60 kg (132 lbs)

Coach:
André Brunet

Category:
Men's singles

Status:
Amateur, France

Highlights

1st at French Championships (1995)

3rd at Olympic Games (1994)

2nd at World Championships (1994)

5th at World Championships (1993)

2nd at European Championships (1993)

9th at World Championships (1992)

5th at European Championships (1991, 1994)

4th at World Junior Championships (1990)

Did you know that . . . ?
The friction of your blade on the ice melts the surface ever so slightly, so when you're skating you're actually sliding on water.

Lu Chen

LU CHEN

National champion at the age of 10 — and reigning national champion for the next eight years running — Lu Chen is China's first really great figure skater. (Until the early 1980s there were no figure skaters in China at all, because there were no covered rinks and no skating coaches!)

In a country where few could skate as well as she could, Lu's challenge to try harder, more complex moves came from herself. "When she was nine years old she achieved the triple jump," her coach says. "At that time, no one in China could make a triple jump, and in fact, at that age, it is not good to teach them that kind of complex movement because they could easily be hurt."

But there was no stopping Lu. Though her program was criticized for not having enough sparkle, Lu became the first Chinese skater ever to win a medal at the World Championships, in 1992. Judges really liked Lu's strong but fluid style and the way she used her arms and upper body in her routines.

In addition to the things she has learned from her coach and choreographer, Li Ming Zhu, Lu has learned much about skating from watching videotapes of her idol, Kristi Yamaguchi. But although she has always wanted to compete with Kristi in the rink, Lu never planned to join her in the professional world of ice shows and advertising. In the remote village in northeastern China where Lu grew up, these opportunities just didn't exist!

In one interview, Lu's coach explained that Lu's skating ability comes from something called *bing gan*, which means a feeling for skating. Now that she's retired from amateur competition, we can only wait to see where Lu's *bing gan* will lead her.

Did you know that . . . ?
Another 10-year-old national champion was Sonja Henie of Norway. During her amateur skating career she won three Olympic golds, *and* the world championship 10 years in a row. Her dazzling success made figure skating hugely popular, and Sonja then went on to Hollywood to become a film star.

Born:
November 4, 1976

In:
Chang Chun, China

Height:
161 cm (5′4″)

Weight:
49 kg (108 lbs)

Coach:
Li Ming Zhu

Category:
Ladies' singles

Status:
Professional

Highlights

3rd at Olympic Games (1994)

3rd at World Championships (1992, 1993)

3rd at World Junior Championships (1992)

6th at Olympic Games (1992)

12th at World Championships (1991)

1st at Chinese Championships (1987, 1988, 1989, 1990, 1991, 1992, 1993, 1994)

Josée Chouinard

JOSÉE CHOUINARD

Three-time national champion Josée Chouinard is an exciting skater with strong jumps and some of the best spins in the business! After her first thrilling gold at the Canadian Championships in 1991, many people hoped that Josée would be the first Canadian woman since Elizabeth Manley to achieve great amateur success on an international level. So not only Josée was disappointed when she failed to win any medals at all at the Albertville Olympics and 1992 World Championships.

Hopes were high again after the 1993 Canadians, where Josée won her second gold. But again, she failed to medal at the World Championships. It was time to make some decisions.

"I was really determined, it was either I quit or I give more than 100 percent. So I decided to sacrifice a little bit more — my friends, my family — and I went away to train. I worked really hard; every time I didn't feel like working out I would say, 'I'm in Toronto for one reason: to train and to accomplish a goal that I've given myself.' "

Josée moved to coach Louis Stong, who also coached her biggest rival, Karen Preston. And although she did win an incredible *third* Canadian title in 1994, medals at the Olympics and World Championships were just out of reach for Josée. She comments on her year of intense training, "It was worth it, but it didn't work out at the end. I was kind of upset and I was blaming it on everything, but then I thought maybe I shouldn't blame it on anything except me."

Abandoning skating altogether was not an option for Josée, though. "I'd miss it too much. So then I made another decision: I went professional."

But after just one year with the ice shows, Josée was ready for competition again. Her amateur status was reinstated on July 1, 1995. Can a skater really come back from retirement and skate to win? The answer must be yes. Josée has already medaled at the 1996 Canadians and continues to thrill fans around the world.

Did you know that . . . ?
Ottawa's Barbara Ann Scott won the first Canadian gold in figure skating at the 1948 Olympics. In fact, she was the first North American to take the title of world champion away from the Europeans.

Born:
August 21, 1969

In:
Rosemont, Quebec

Height:
155 cm (5'2")

Weight:
49 kg (108 lbs)

Coach:
Louis Stong

Category:
Ladies' singles

Status:
Amateur, Canada

Highlights

2nd at Canadian Championships (1996)

9th at Olympic Games (1994)

5th at World Championships (1992, 1994)

9th at Olympic Games (1992)

6th at World Championships (1991)

1st at Canadian Championships (1991, 1993, 1994)

3rd at Canadian Championships (1990)

7th at Canadian Championships (1989)

Susan Humphreys

SUSAN HUMPHREYS

The youngest of four children in a family of skaters, Susan Humphreys put on her first pair of skates at the age of three. But she didn't begin to take her sport seriously until shoulder surgery kept her off the ice for four months when she was 15. "It was at that point that I decided I wanted to work hard for it," says Susan.

And work hard she does. In addition to the 16 hours a week Susan works on the ice, she spends many more hours off the ice, lifting weights, doing aerobics to build stamina, and perfecting her movements with her ballet and jazz teachers.

Susan admits it can be tough to stay with her program from late October right through to March. "It's hard to discipline yourself to go in and do it every day. By the end of the week you're tired, and when the next week starts you're still tired from the week before, and that goes on and on. By the end of the season you're just wiped out."

At the 1994 Canadian Championships, Susan surprised everyone by taking second place and a spot on the team going to the Winter Olympics. But her performance at the Olympics was anything but thrilling — Susan was eliminated in the preliminaries, coming in 26th place out of 27 skaters. She had all kinds of problems that day, but the worst was when she fell on the last jump in her program. Susan says, "A double Lutz is really easy for me; I've been doing that since I was 11 years old. I went up into it and I came down, and all of a sudden I was on the ice!"

Despite the shaking this gave her confidence, Susan stayed focused and went on to finish ninth at her first-ever Worlds. "I skated the best I ever have in the competition, in both programs. For me it was overcoming my fear of failure. Of course, I'm probably going to feel that sometime again, but for this year it was a lot for me to prove to myself I could go out there and do it, and feel like I really belonged."

Born:
October 30, 1975

In:
Moose Jaw,
Saskatchewan

Height:
165 cm (5′6″)

Weight:
54 kg (118 lbs)

Coach:
Christy Ness

Category:
Ladies' singles

Status:
Amateur, Canada

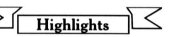

9th at World
Championships
(1994)

2nd at Canadian
Championships
(1994)

3rd at Canadian
Championships
(1993, 1995, 1996)

Did you know that . . . ?
**At the 1962 World Championships in Prague,
Canadian Donald Jackson did the first triple Lutz
ever in competition.**

Nancy Kerrigan

NANCY KERRIGAN

With her name in news headlines around the world, the 1994 Olympics were probably the hardest competition Nancy Kerrigan has ever had to face.

In fact, Nancy was afraid she wouldn't even be allowed to skate, because according to U.S. Figure Skating Association rules, only skaters who have skated medal-winning performances in the U.S. Championships or in the previous year's World Championships are even considered for the U.S. Olympic team.

Nancy, of course, missed the national championships that year after being clubbed in the knee by an intruder at the competition. And at the World Championships in 1993 she had skated one of the worst performances of her life.

Luckily, an exception to the rule was made and Nancy was invited to join the 1994 Olympic Team because of special circumstances.

At Lillehammer, Nancy skated the best she ever has in competition, once and for all overcoming her reputation for freezing under pressure. In what some people believed to be a controversial decision, Nancy won the silver medal, narrowly losing the gold to Ukrainian skater Oksana Baiul.

The youngest of three children, Nancy is very considerate of her mother, who suffers from a condition called multiple neuritis which has made her legally blind. So that her mother can see how they will look, Nancy walks through her routines in the family's living room. And whenever possible she selects skating costumes that will be easy for her mother to see from a distance. During an interview, Nancy told one reporter, "My mother can't see with the clarity you and I have, but she's such an inspiration for me to skate well."

School is so important.
Skating isn't everything. I see kids so
absorbed in it. Your body can't last forever,
but your mind does. So you need
an education.

— Nancy

Born:
October 13, 1969

In:
Woburn,
Massachusetts, USA

Height:
163 cm (5′4″)

Weight:
52 kg (115 lbs)

Coach:
Evy and Mary
Scotvold

Category:
Ladies' singles

Status:
Professional

Highlights

2nd at Olympic
Games (1994)

1st at U.S.
Championships
(1993)

2nd at World
Championships
(1992)

3rd at Olympic
Games (1992)

2nd at U.S.
Championships
(1992)

3rd at World
Championships
(1991)

Michelle Kwan

MICHELLE KWAN

As the last of three children, Michelle Kwan is an expert at being the youngest, off and on the ice. She was the youngest skating champion ever at the 1993 U.S. Olympic Festival, the 1995 Nations Cup and Skate America 1994. In 1996 Michelle became the youngest-ever U.S. national champion.

How did she get to be so good so fast? Sheer determination. Michelle began skating at the age of five and by the time she was six had decided she wanted to win a gold medal at the Olympic Games.

By 1992, Michelle was 9th at the Junior Nationals. It wasn't a great placing, but it was enough to make Michelle want to take her senior level test. Never mind that her coach didn't think she was ready. Michelle just waited until he was out of town and signed up for the test herself.

Incredibly, twelve-year-old Michelle actually passed, and in under a year landed six triple jumps at the 1993 Olympic Festival to win!

Michelle's next brush with fame came a year later when she was second at the U.S. championships. That should have earned her a position on the Olympic team, but she lost her spot to Nancy Kerrigan. Michelle went to Lillehammer as an alternate, but did not compete. It was a major disappointment.

But pressure doesn't seem to bother Michelle. Only months after the rollercoaster ride of the '94 Olympics, she skated what *Skating Magazine* called "the single greatest performance of the season" at the 1994 Worlds.

What does Michelle think is hard about skating? "I guess I miss some of my school friends, but we still keep in touch. We write letters... I do a lot of things with my friends up at Ice Castle. We go to the movies, hang out. You know. The only things I don't do are skiing or sky diving! Something dangerous. I don't want to have an injury."

You have to put this in perspective. There are going to be ups and downs. It's easy to be on the podium, but you have to learn how to lose. If she skates for 10 years — 70 competitions and shows a year — that's 700 performances she has left. You can't get crazy over one of them.

— Michelle's dad

Born:
Born: July 7, 1980

In:
Torrance, CA

Height:
160 cm (5'2")

Weight:
43 kg (96 lbs)

Coach:
Frank Carroll

Category:
Ladies' singles

Status:
Amateur,
United States

Highlights

1st at U.S.
Championships
(1996)

4th at World
Championships
(1995)

2nd at U.S.
Championships
(1995, 1994)

8th at World
Championships
(1994)

1st at Junior World
Championships
(1994)

6th at U.S.
Championships
(1993)

9th at U.S.
Championships
(1992)

Jennifer Robinson

JENNIFER ROBINSON

It was the dazzle of flashy skating costumes and the cheers of an Ice Capades crowd that made an eight-year-old Jennifer Robinson quit gymnastics and take up figure skating.

Jennifer remembers, "It looked really glamorous, and I was really horrid at gymnastics."

However awkward Jennifer may have felt on land, she's certainly become a graceful presence in the rink. More than a decade after deciding she "wanted to make the Olympics in something," this is one Canadian skater who just might get her wish.

"I was kind of a fast learner, I guess. When I was a little kid I really liked to show off. I used to like to dance for my parents in the living room, and when I got on the ice it just seemed like that."

In a way, showing off has become one of Jennifer's strengths in the rink. She isn't nervous about performing for crowds and she doesn't take herself or her work too seriously.

"I'm very competitive by nature, but I don't really think of what I do as a job. I have a lot of fun skating and I think that's why I am still skating. I like the crowds and I love how fast I skate."

Does Jennifer have any tricks for staying calm under all that pressure? "When I go to bed on nights before I compete, I sleep in an air position with my feet crossed and my arms pulled in. It helps me relax."

And, of course, training twenty-five to thirty-five hours a week hasn't hurt either. It's won Jennifer her first major prize — the 1996 Canadian championship.

Jennifer's advice to skaters? "Be silly. I've been here for three years and training sometimes gets pretty intense. You want to do your best and you're trying to relax. Sometimes you've got to do something to release the tension, so you tell jokes."

Be yourself and have a total blast with what you're doing. I know that sounds really clichéd, but it's true. If you're not having fun you're not going to learn as fast. That's probably what's going to get you the furthest.
— Jennifer

Born:
December 2, 1976

In:
Goderich, Ontario

Height:
167 cm (5'7")

Weight:
57 kg (125 lbs)

Coaches:
Doug Leigh,
Robert Tebby

Category:
Ladies' singles

Status:
Amateur, Canada

Highlights

1st at Canadian
Championships
(1996)

19th at World
Championships
(1995)

2nd at Canadian
Championships
(1995)

1st at Canadian
Junior
Championships
(1994)

Sargeant / Wirtz

KRISTY SARGEANT
and
KRIS WIRTZ

With names like Kris and Kristy it seems like this team was made for each other. They certainly got together quickly enough! Kris recalls that five months after breaking up with his first skating partner he was ready to skate with someone new. "Kristy's name came up and three days after I phoned her, she was here!" he exclaims.

But still, Kris and Kristy say that it took them about a year, practicing together and separately under the direction of their coach Paul Wirtz (who also happens to be Kris's brother), to develop the trust they need to compete in the most dangerous kind of figure skating of all.

After finishing a disappointing fifth at their first Canadian Championships in 1993, the pair went through a pretty tough time. Kris says, "It was really depressing and we were considering if we even wanted to do it anymore."

But there was at least one reason to keep going: Kris had competed in the 1992 Winter Olympic Games. "I knew what it was like, and I knew what it would be like just to watch it on TV — it would hurt a lot. So we said, 'To heck with it, let's do it! Let's be the best we can!' "

Determination paid off. They took second place at the 1994 Canadian Championships in Edmonton to secure a position on Canada's Olympic team. (Of course, the fact that Kristy's hometown crowd was there in full force to cheer them on helped!)

Today they don't ever let themselves get that discouraged. Their observations after going to their first Olympics? "It's a great team thing. It's not about yourself. You feel good whether you win or lose because somebody on your team is going to make you proud for Canada. You like to be out there representing the country."

Sport is easy once you really learn to enjoy it. If you're just doing it because your mother wants you to or because everybody else is doing it, it's not going to be anything special. Whatever you do, enjoy doing it and you'll become part of it.
— Kristy and Kris

Born:
January 24, 1974
December 12, 1969

In:
Red Deer, Alberta
Fort William,
Ontario

Height:
150 cm (5′)
168 cm (5′7″)

Weight:
46 kg (102 lbs)
70 kg (155 lbs)

Coach:
Paul Wirtz

Category:
Pairs

Status:
Amateur, Canada

Highlights

2nd at Canadian
Championships
(1996)

11th at World
Championships
(1994)

10th at Olympic
Games (1994)

2nd at Canadian
Championships
(1994)

5th at Canadian
Championships
(1993, 1995)

Elvis Stojko

ELVIS STOJKO

Just like the famous singer he was named after, Elvis Stojko is a big talent with lots of flash — and lots of fans!

A dirt biker with a black belt in karate, Elvis is not what you would call a flowery skater. He is also not what you would call a traditional skater; Elvis performed his short program at the 1994 Olympic Games in a studded leather outfit his mother made for him. And he skated a powerful, action-packed long program that was full of kung fu moves.

While audiences love Elvis's spectacular skating, many judges still prefer to see something that looks a lot more like ballet on ice. And it shows in the marks they've been giving skaters like Elvis. Asked to comment on Elvis's electric performance at Lillehammer, coach Doug Leigh told one reporter, "They [Elvis and equally creative bronze medalist Philippe Candeloro] wear their own shoes. At least these guys stepped forward with a refreshing change. The judges should be open to the other flavours that are out there."

Just the same, Elvis has been working with choreographer Uschi Keszler to add some form to his otherwise powerful performances. Elvis knows this can only help him so much, because he isn't built like a ballet dancer: he has a muscular upper body and short legs, and all the practice in the world cannot change that. Besides, when you've got a good thing going, why mess with it?

When Doug Leigh first met Elvis, he remembers, "He was small, fast, good, but what impressed me most was the direct way he'd look at you." It's that iron determination that has carried this skater through the challenges of fractured bones and stiff competition.

Says Elvis, "I guess I just want to be the best. It's the same with the other things I do, like the martial arts or motorbiking. Some days I get bored with training, but that's when I'm not looking for new things to do. I have to set new goals all the time, higher and higher, better and better."

The challenge is not to win but to conquer the fear. It's not the other skaters I have to beat, it's myself.

— Elvis

Born:
March 22, 1972

In:
Newmarket, Ontario

Height:
168 cm (5'7")

Weight:
69 kg (152 lbs)

Coach:
Doug Leigh

Category:
Men's singles

Status:
Amateur, Canada

Highlights

1st at World Championships (1994, 1995)

2nd at Olympic Games (1994)

1st at Canadian Championships (1994, 1996)

2nd at World Championships (1993)

2nd at Canadian Championships (1990, 1991, 1992, 1993)

6th at World Championships (1991)

9th at World Championships (1990)

Alexei Urmanov

ALEXEI URMANOV

Who claimed the gold at the 1994 Winter Olympic Games? It wasn't previous gold medalists Brian Boitano or Viktor Petrenko. To the disappointment of many Canadians it wasn't even Alberta's showman on skates, four-time world champion Kurt Browning.

No, the skater who did it was Russia's Alexei Urmanov. Next to the bronze medal he won at the 1993 Worlds, it was his first important international win, ever! And he did it skating against some of the toughest competitors ever to meet on Olympic ice.

After his surprise finish, Alexei was asked if he ever thought he would win the gold at Lillehammer. Urmanov answered in halting English, "I didn't think so. Kurt Browning too strong. Who knows about mistakes of Browning, Petrenko and Boitano in technical [short] program?"

Alexei's coach told one interviewer that Alexei's ability to combine beauty, grace and technique is what makes him an excellent skater. And judges seem to agree. Alexei is tall and powerful, and his long arms and legs allow him to make long clean lines when he moves. He still needs to improve his spins, but his classic style of skating — not to mention his traditional choices in costumes and music — have helped judges overlook this shortcoming.

Like ladies' gold medalist Oksana Baiul, Alexei has had to train under difficult conditions. In Russia he's only able to practice two hours a day, and unlike the $30 000 a year or more that North American coaches make from their skaters, he pays his coach only $30 a month. At one time Alexei even relied on his coach to pay for his costumes! Today, though, with an Olympic gold medal under his belt, Alexei may just have a bigger, brighter future ahead of him.

Did you know that . . . ?
After winning an Olympic medal, most figure skaters turn professional? This means they stop skating in amateur competitions to take high paying jobs with ice shows or as product sponsors. After years of coaching bills and rink fees, this is one opportunity that few skaters can afford to miss!

Born:
November 17, 1973

In:
St. Petersburg, Russia

Height:
182 cm (6′1″)

Weight:
72 kg (158 lbs)

Coach:
Alexei Mishin

Category:
Men's singles

Status:
Amateur, Russia

Highlights

1st in Champions Series (1996)

2nd at European Championships (1995)

4th at World Championships (1994, 1995)

1st at Olympic Games (1994)

3rd at World Championships (1993)

5th at Olympic Games (1992)

3rd at European Championships (1992)

Kristi Yamaguchi

KRISTI YAMAGUCHI

Skating coaches agree that if you want to be good, you have to start young. Well, Kristi Yamaguchi certainly proves that point. She began skating at the tender age of six and was competing by the time she was nine years old!

Though opting to train at Edmonton's Royal Glenora Club, far from her home in Fremont, California, Kristi says she still relied on her family's influence to help her keep things in perspective. Even after medaling in both singles *and* pairs at the 1989 U.S. Championships — the first woman to do so since 1954 — and even after winning back-to-back World Championships in 1991 and 1992, Kristi says her family life never really changed.

Neither Kristi nor her family was expecting her to win much of anything at the 1992 Winter Games. Kristi hadn't quite mastered the triple Axel, a jump that her biggest rival, Midori Ito, had no trouble with. But Kristi's elegance and clean lines won the day. She skated a nearly perfect program, and even without the triple Axel became the first American woman to skate to Olympic gold since Dorothy Hamill in 1976 — a curious coincidence, since Kristi remembers favoring a Dorothy Hamill doll she had when she was five! This win was the second of three golds Kristi would capture that year, thereby completing a 1992 sweep of the Olympics and U.S. and World Championships.

Kristi's decision to turn professional has also been a hit. Her fresh look has found its way into glamorous spreads for *Elle*, *Seventeen* and *Vogue* magazines, and she has scored high marks with advertisers as well. Her professional skating career took off right away, too.

What more could a young skater want?

Did you know that . . .?
The greatest number of perfect scores
ever awarded to a single female skater was seven,
to Japan's Midori Ito at the World Championships
in Paris, France in 1989.

Born:
July 12, 1971

In:
Hayward, California

Height:
152 cm (5′1″)

Weight:
40 kg (88 lbs)

Coach:
Christy Ness

Category:
Ladies' singles

Status:
Professional

Highlights

1st at Olympic Games (1992)

1st at U.S. Championships (1992)

1st at World Championships (1991, 1992)

2nd at U.S. Championships (1990, 1991)

4th at World Championships (1990)

1st at U.S. Championships, pairs (1989)

2nd at U.S. Championships, singles (1989)

∞ ABOUT THE EVENTS ∞

Singles and Pairs Skating

In both the singles and pairs events, skaters must perform two routines, a short program (also called a technical program) and a long program (also called a freestyle program).

In the short program athletes must complete eight required moves in a choreographed routine lasting no longer than two minutes and 40 seconds. The long program is four minutes long for women and four and a half minutes long for men, and has no required moves. The short program score counts for one third of the final mark, the long program counts for the remaining two thirds.

Ice Dancing

In ice dancing there are three parts to the competition: two compulsory dances, an original dance and a free dance.

In their compulsories, skaters must perform a specified series of moves to a particular type of dance. In the original dance portion, only the type of dance is specified. In the free dance, skaters are allowed to select their own type of dance, music and choreography.

What about figures?

When figure skating first began, the emphasis was on performing figures, or tracing shapes on the ice. This wasn't very exciting to watch, though, and over the years the figures were made to count less and less. Now they have been eliminated completely from competiton.

∞ ABOUT THE JUDGING ∞

After their performance, skaters get two separate marks from judges, one for technical merit and another for presentation. Here's what those marks mean:

0.0	1.0	2.0	3.0	4.0	5.0	6.0
not skated	very poor	poor	mediocre	good	very good	perfect and faultless

Scoring is done by tenths of a point. So, if a skater gets a mark of 5.5, for example, that means the performance was half-way between being very good and perfect.

Technical Merit

To award high marks for technical merit, judges want to see a difficult program with no mistakes. Obviously skaters lose marks for falling, but they can also lose marks for other, harder-to-see errors. Here's what judges look for:

Jumps

Jumps are marked on how difficult they are. A triple jump, for example, is more difficult to do than a double or a single jump. Judges also look at how fast skaters perform their jumps and how clean their take-offs and landings are. Jumps should be landed solidly on one foot with the other leg well extended, and a good landing should be held for a few seconds to show control. When skaters do combination jumps (one after the other) they get higher marks from the judges.

Spins

The challenge of a good spin is to keep the centre of rotation over one spot on the ice, not letting it "travel" in any direction. Faster spins, and spins in different positions, are more difficult and will get higher marks.

Step sequences

Footwork connects all of the other elements in a program. A step sequence is a section of footwork which takes a particular shape: straight, circular, serpentine (S-shaped) or spiral. The footwork should be fast and intricate, and often includes moves such as spread eagles.

Presentation

Presentation marks reflect the overall performance of a skater. Judges will ask themselves questions like:

- ✓ How creatively did the skaters perform during the time available?
- ✓ Did they make good use of all the ice surface?
- ✓ Was each element of the program connected smoothly to the others?
- ✓ How well did they express the character of the music?
- ✓ Did they skate in time to the music?
- ✓ Did they appear to skate with ease and with speed?
- ✓ How original and interesting was the performance?

How it all goes together

Each judge provides two marks for performance — technical and presentation — which are added together. This combined mark is used to rank each skater according to how well he or she did compared to the other competitors. The rankings of the individual judges are called ordinals. The skater who gets the most first-place ordinals is declared the winner of the competition.

∽MORE ABOUT SKATING∽

Skates

Skating is probably the world's oldest winter sport. The first skates were animal bones, ground flat on one side and strapped to the feet with leather thongs. Skating was born in Scandinavia in the eighth century or earlier, and spread through northern Europe over the next few hundred years. In the Netherlands, the skate picked up its English name: the word "skate" comes from the Dutch word "schaat," which means bone.

Rinks

The world's first indoor, artificially frozen ice rink was the Glaciarium of London, England, built in 1876. This invention meant that skating could change from a winter pasttime to a major sport.

Figure skating

Figure skating was a stiff, awkward sport until American Jackson Haines (1840-1876) tried it. Haines was a ballet master who combined dance moves with skating. His new, free style didn't catch on right away in America or England, but he was an instant success in Vienna, where he taught the Viennese to waltz on ice. Today Haines is known as the "father of figure skating."

Figure skating became a regular part of the Olympic Games in 1908. Ice dancing wasn't added to the Winter Olympic program until 1976.

∽FOR MORE INFORMATION∽

Books

Canada at the Olympic Winter Games by Wendy Bryden. Hurtig Publishers Ltd., 1987.
The Complete Book of the Winter Olympics by David Wallechinsky. Little, Brown & Company, 1993.
The Kids Guide to the 1994 Winter Olympics by Stephen Malley. Bantam Books, 1994.
Kurt: Forcing the Edge by Kurt Browning. HarperCollins Publishers Ltd., 1991.
Let the Games Begin by Randy Starkman. Scholastic Canada Ltd., 1994.
Nancy Kerrigan: Heart of a Champion by Mikki Morrissette. Bantam Books, 1994.
The Olympic Factbook by Martin Connors, Diane Dupuis, Marie J. MacNee and Christa Brelin. Visible Ink Press, 1984.

Magazines

Blades On Ice, Blades On Ice Inc., 7040 North Mona Lisa Road, Tucson, AZ 85741-2633 USA.
International Figure Skating, Paragraph Communications, L.P., 55 Ideal Road, Worcestershire, MA 01604 USA.
Today's Skater, National All-Sport Promotions, a division of St. Clair Group Investments Inc., Suite #805, 30 St. Clair Avenue West, Toronto, ON M4V 3A1.

Organizations

The United States Figure Skating Association, 20 First Street, Colorado Springs, CO 80906 USA.

📬 Where To Send Your Fan Mail

Oksana Baiul
International Skating Union
c/o Member Club
Information
Promenade 73
Postfach CH 7270
Davos Platz, Switzerland

**Shae-Lynn Bourne and
Victor Kraatz**
Mentor Marketing
c/o Ed Futerman
2 St. Clair Avenue East
15th floor, Colonial Tower
Toronto, ON
M4T 2R1

**Isabelle Brasseur and
Lloyd Eisler**
International
Management Group
c/o Yuki Saegusa
22 East 71st Street
New York, NY
USA 10021

Sébastien Britten
c/o Canadian Figure
Skating Association
1600 James Naismith Drive
Gloucester, ON
K1B 5N4

Kurt Browning
International
Management Group
c/o Kevin Albrecht
1 St. Clair Avenue East
Suite # 700
Toronto, ON
M4T 2V7

Philippe Candeloro
Candeloro International
Sport Management
22 avenue des Renouillers
92 700 Colombes
France

Lu Chen
International
Management Group
c/o Jay Ogden/Yuki
Saegusa
22 East 71st Street
New York, NY
USA 10021

Josée Chouinard
International
Management Group
c/o Kevin Albrecht
1 St. Clair Avenue East
Suite # 700
Toronto, ON
M4T 2V7

Susan Humphreys
c/o Canadian Figure
Skating Association
1600 James Naismith Drive
Gloucester, ON
K1B 5N4

Nancy Kerrigan
c/o USFSA
20 First St.
Colorado Springs, CO
USA 80906

Michelle Kwan
c/o USFSA
20 First St.
Colorado Springs, CO
USA 80906

Jennifer Robinson
c/o Canadian Figure
Skating Association
1600 James Naismith Drive
Gloucester, ON
K1B 5N4

**Kristy Sargeant and
Kris Wirtz**
c/o Canadian Figure
Skating Association
1600 James Naismith Drive
Gloucester, ON
K1B 5N4

Elvis Stojko
Mentor Marketing
c/o Ed Futerman
2 St. Clair Avenue East
15th floor, Colonial Tower
Toronto, ON
M4T 2R1

Alexei Urmanov
International Skating Union
c/o Member Club
Information
Promenade 73
Postfach CH 7270
Davos Platz,
Switzerland

Kristi Yamaguchi
International
Management Group
c/o Kevin Albrecht
1 St. Clair Avenue East
Suite # 700
Toronto, ON
M4T 2V7

Try surfing the Net for home pages for your favorite skaters. Just do a web search by name.